WOULD YOU RATHER

CHRISTMAS EDITION

Flyer.Prod

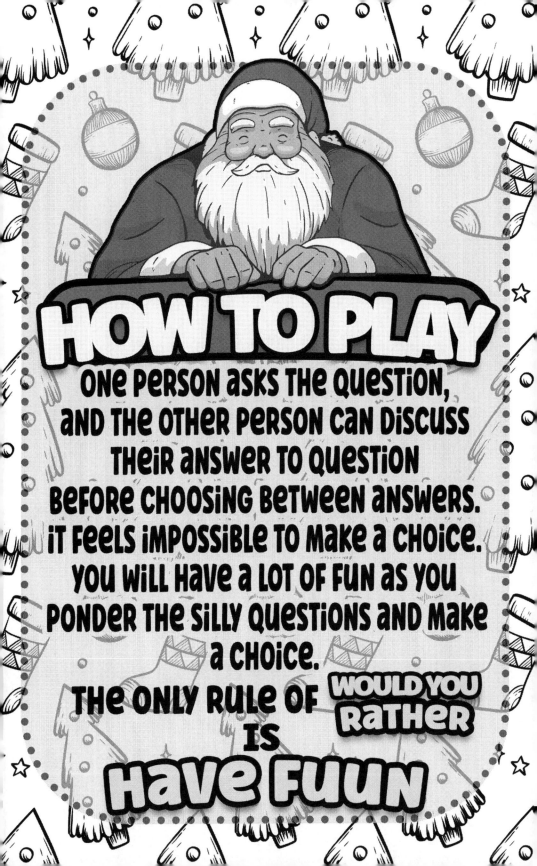

HOW TO PLAY

ONE PERSON ASKS THE QUESTION, AND THE OTHER PERSON CAN DISCUSS THEIR ANSWER TO QUESTION BEFORE CHOOSING BETWEEN ANSWERS. IT FEELS IMPOSSIBLE TO MAKE A CHOICE. YOU WILL HAVE A LOT OF FUN AS YOU PONDER THE SILLY QUESTIONS AND MAKE A CHOICE. THE ONLY RULE OF WOULD YOU RATHER IS HAVE FUUN

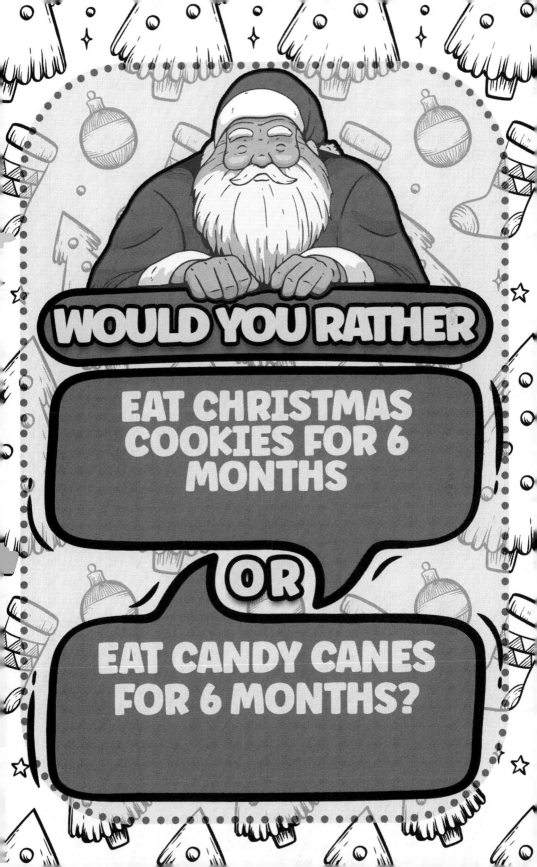

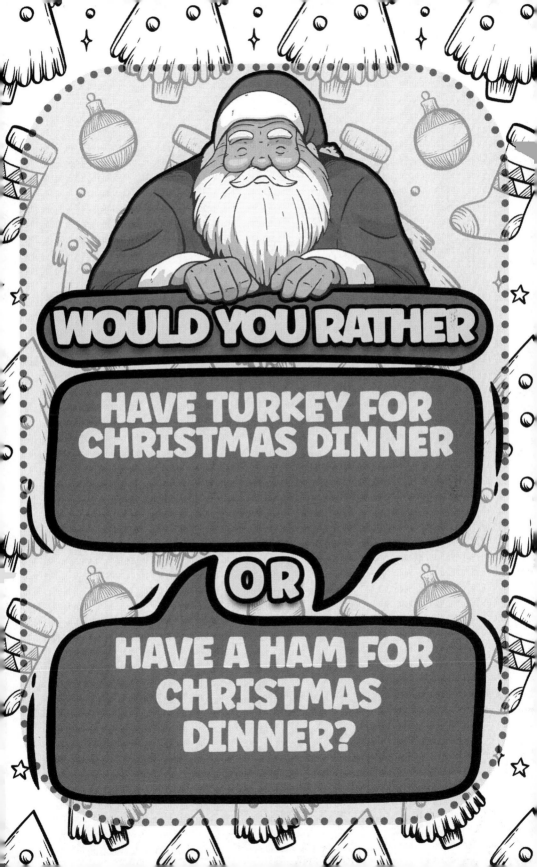

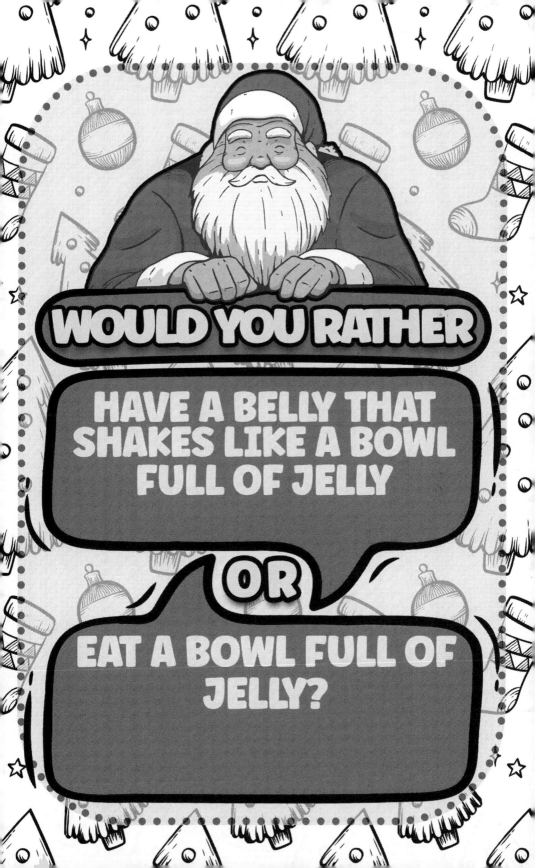

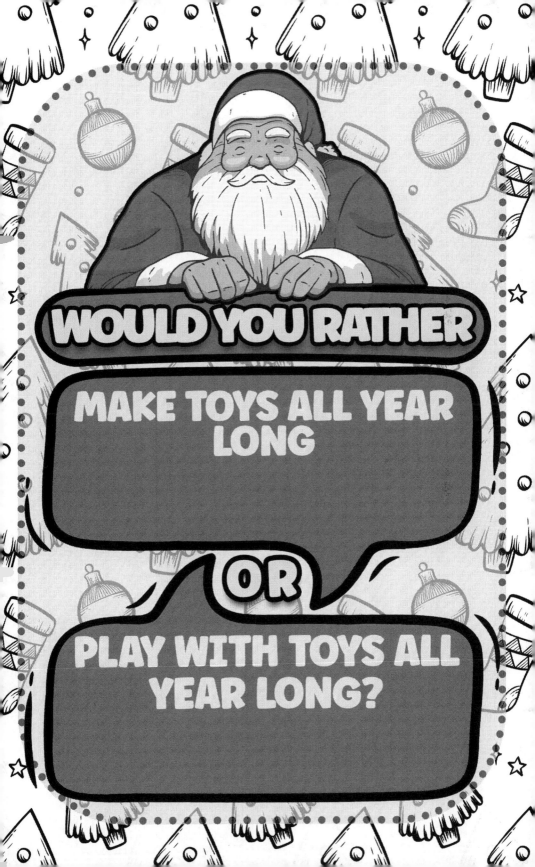

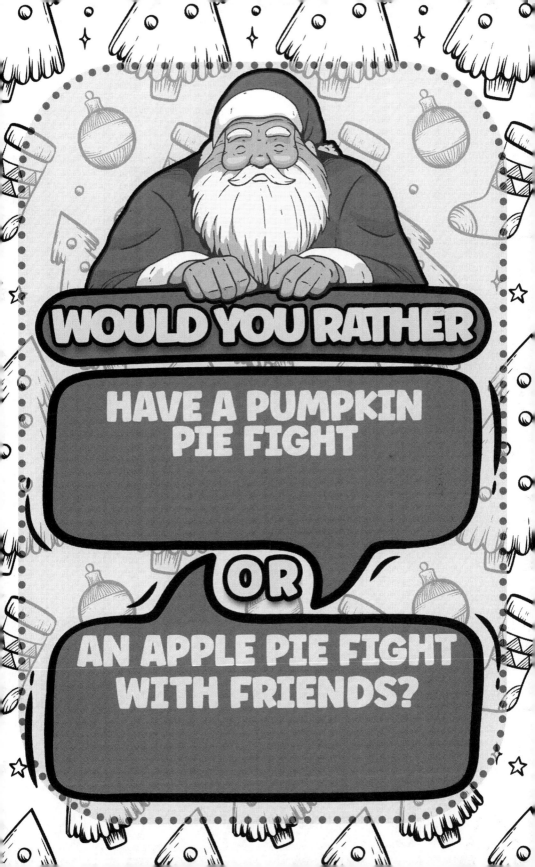

WOULD YOU RATHER

HAVE ELF EARS

OR

A SANTA BEARD?

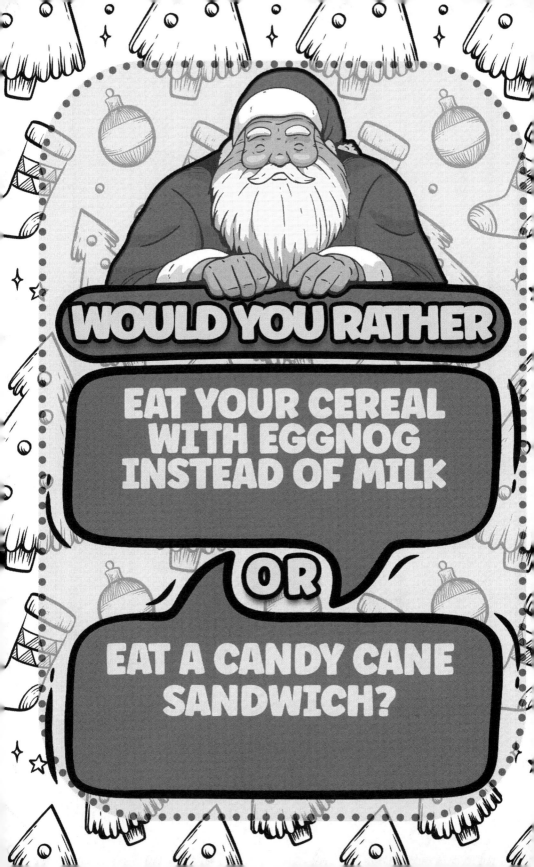

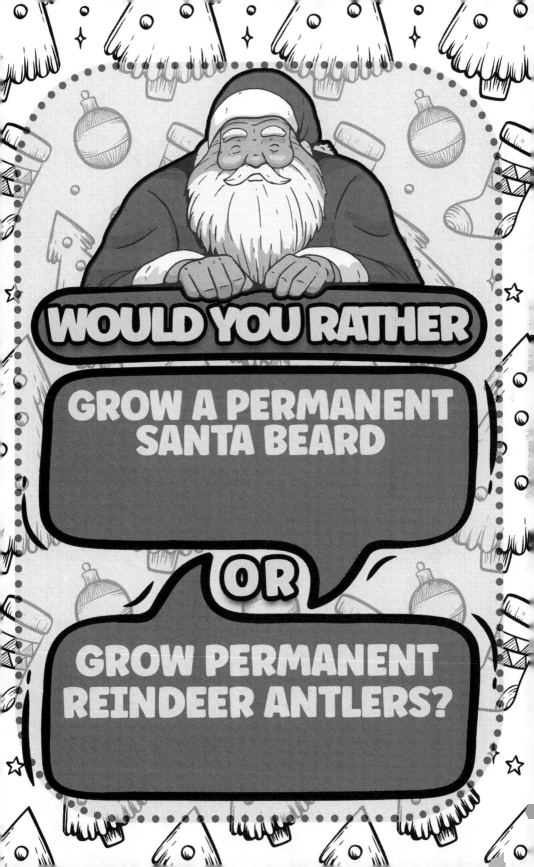

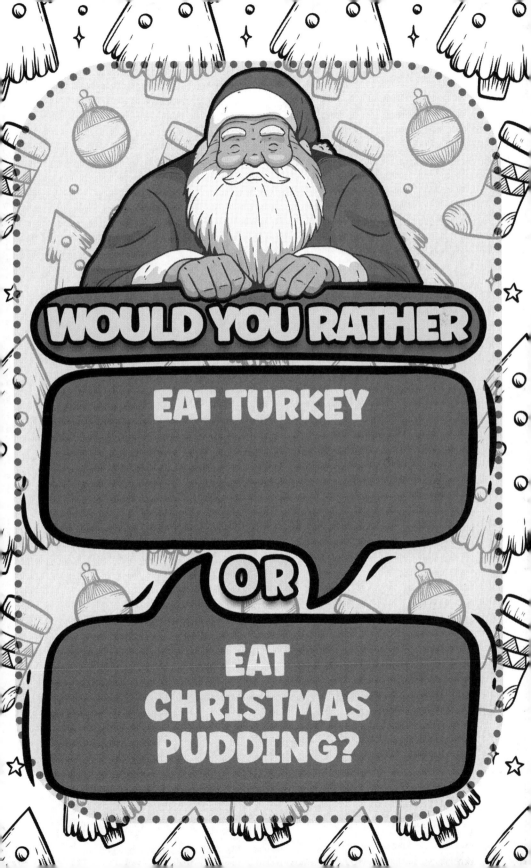

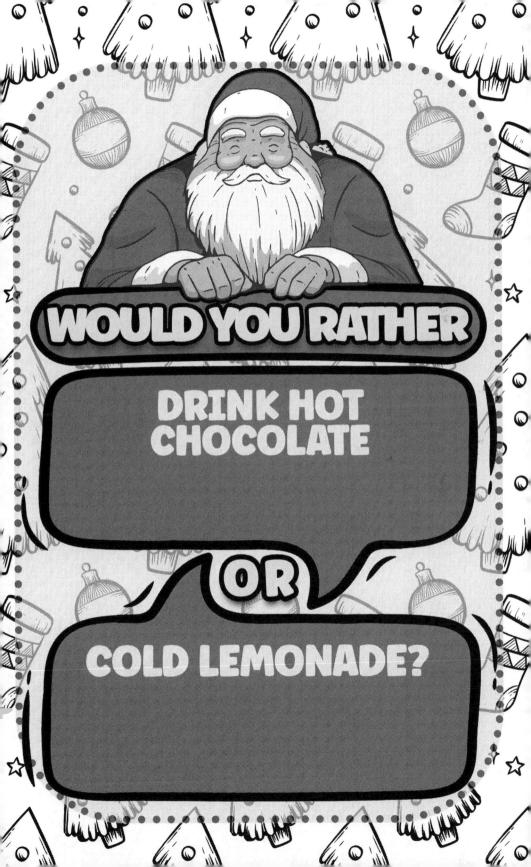

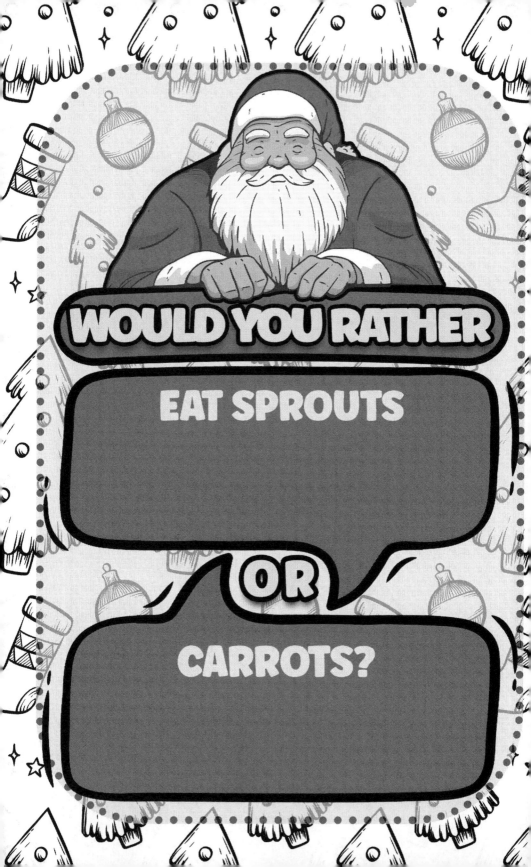

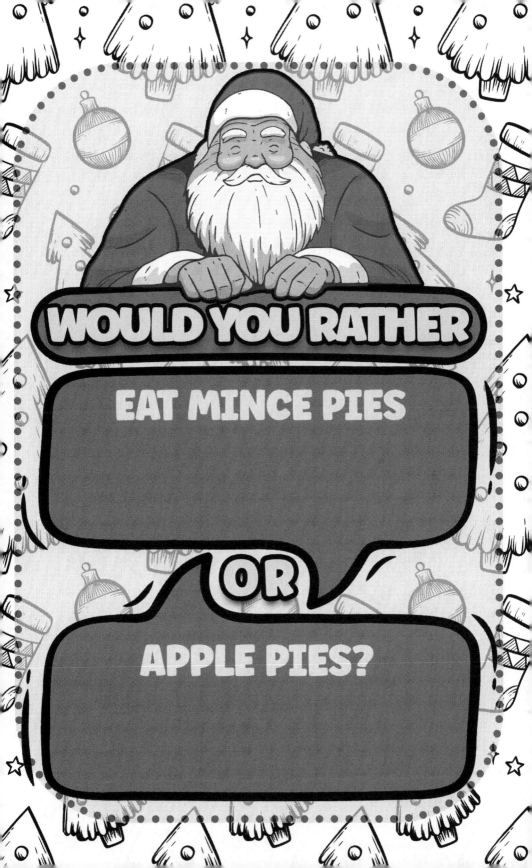

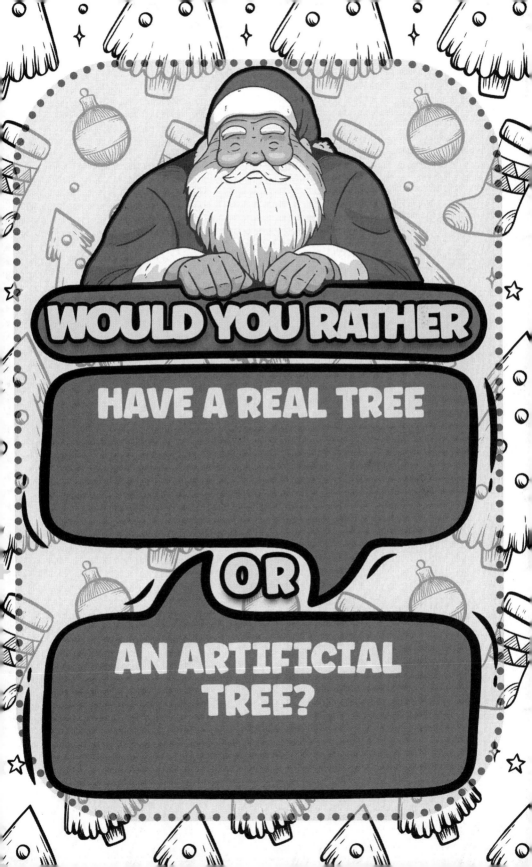

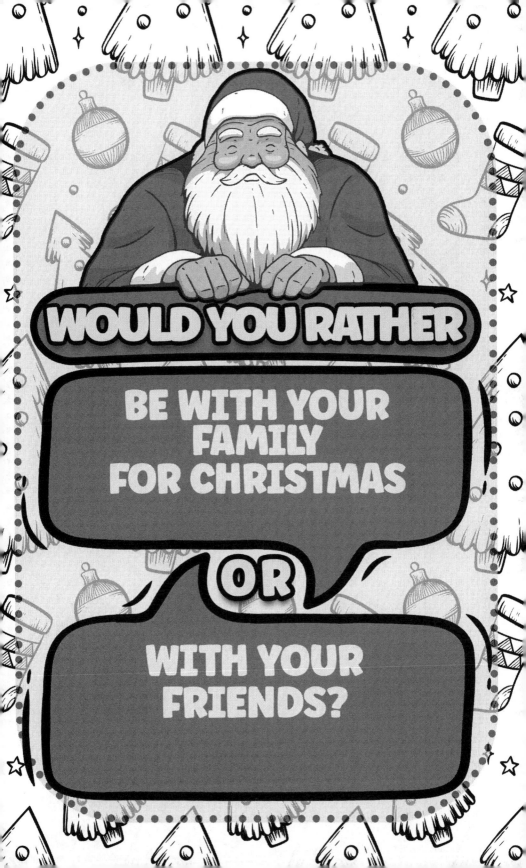

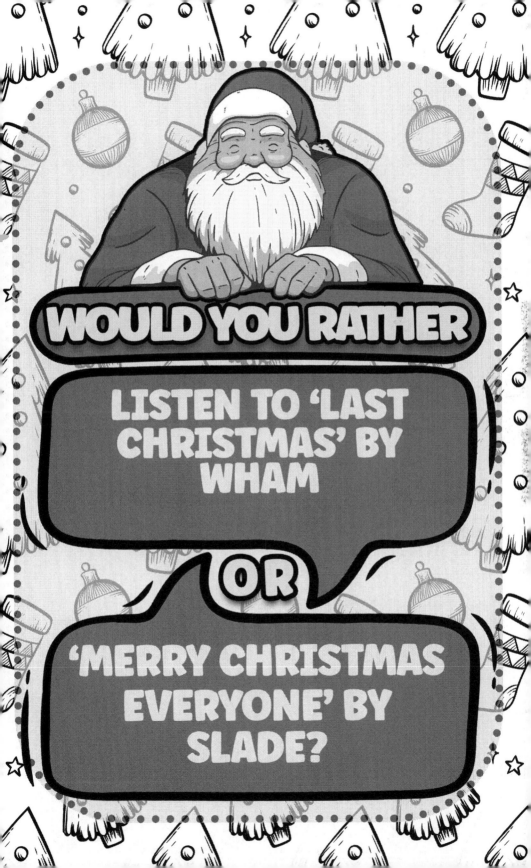

30963612R00057